The mus

This is a book of jokes well past their sell-by date. If you find you recognise one or more of these jokes, you probably told it to me some time in the 1950s.

Does it contain adult humour? Of course not. I spent 32 years teaching adolescents. It contains a small amount of adolescent humour – generally intended to shock adults.
If you enjoy the book, please write a favourable review on Amazon. If you don't enjoy it – we'll just keep it between ourselves shall we?

Derek McMillan

Johnson, Clegg and Blair

This joke was certainly made about Margaret Thatcher and once about Benjamin Disraeli, it was probably made about Julius Caesar

> Boris Johnson went on a visit to the Zoo. Nobody was talking to him so he stopped to chat with the boa constrictor.

The zoo keeper said "Why are you talking to that disgusting reptile."

Johnson started to look pumped up and responded,

"I am the Prime Minister, I talk to who I like."

The zoo keeper responded, "I was talking to the boa constrictor, who the Hell are you?"

Umbulla

Blair visited Kenya. While there he stopped off to talk to local villagers. His guide assured him that he would have a great reception and sure enough every soundbite was greeted by villagers chanting "Umbulla! Umbulla!"

Enthusiastically he agreed to go to another village with his guide. And again he was greeted with cries of "Umbulla! Umbulla!"

All would have been well had he not seen some villagers tending cattle and suggested to his guide that he should go and talk to them.

Without thinking his guide confided, "No you don't want to go in that field. The cattle have been there a while and you will be up to your neck in umbulla."

Clegg

Clegg died ... no wait stop laughing, there's more.

It seems that he had done some good deeds in his life before he became a politician. Then he was seduced by the dark side of the force or David Cameron as he is known.

Well for St Peter this was a problem and he explained that although he deserved to enter because of the good things in his life this was exactly balanced by the bad.

So he showed him a vision. In this vision Clegg was surrounded by beautiful women whose sole purpose was to keep him happy.

Then he showed him a vision of Hell in which again Clegg was surrounded by beautiful women whose sole purpose was to keep him happy.

Confused, he turned to St Peter who explained, "You see up here, you are being rewarded, down there they are being punished.

GCSE howlers (allegedly)

The following questions and answers were collated from last year's British GCSE exams.

Q. Explain one of the processes by which water can be made safe to drink.
A: Flirtation makes water safe to drink because it removes large pollutants like grit, sand, dead sheep and canoeists.

Q: How is dew formed?
A: The sun shines down on the leaves and makes them perspire.

Q: What causes the tides in the oceans?
A: All water tends to flow towards the moon, because there is no water on the moon, and nature abhors a vacuum.

Sociology Q: What guarantees may a mortgage company insist on?
A: If you are buying a house, they will insist you are well endowed.

Biology Q: What happens to your body as you age?
A: When you get old, so do your bowels and you get intercontinental.

Q: What happens to a boy when he reaches puberty?
A: He says goodbye to his boyfriend and looks forward to his adultery.

Q: Name a major disease associated with cigarettes?
A: Premature death.

Q: How can you delay milk turning sour?
A. Keep it in the cow.

Q: What does "varicose" mean?
A: Nearby.

Q: What is the most common form of birth control?
A: Most people prevent contraception by wearing a condominium.

Q: Give an example of a fungus. What is a characteristic feature?
A: Mushrooms. They always grow in damp places and so they look like umbrellas.

At the intergalactic hotel

(Warning 1 only mathematicians find this remotely funny)

(Warning 2 I really do mean remotely!)

The Intergalactic Hotel has an infinite number of rooms. Unfortunately when I arrived there was a conference with delegates from all over the galaxy, from the infinite star systems.

The receptionist had to inform me that with an infinite number of rooms and an infinite number of guests, there was no room for me.

I was very worried about this, as I had nowhere else to go. Fortunately I spotted a mathematician from Sirius and asked him for a solution to the problem.

He looked at me as if I were a very lowly form of life - but Sirians don't have another way of looking at people unfortunately - and told the receptionist that he could put me in room number 1 and move all the other guests up one.

(Warning 3 I was not kidding was I?)

Kashmir

A woman is arrested on the border of Kashmir. After the police have gone through the usual procedures, a policeman pulls a very large gun and pops the question:

"So are you a Hindu or a Moslem?"

In a cunning bid to keep alive she says she is an atheist.

The policeman thinks (clearly a painful process for him). Then he points the gun at her again.

"So are you a Hindu atheist or a Moslem atheist?"

No worries

If you are alive you only have two worries.

Are you rich or are you poor?

If you are rich you have no worries.

If you are poor you only have two worries.

Are you healthy or are you unhealthy?

If you are healthy you have no worries.

If you are unhealthy you only have two worries.

Will you live or will you die?

If you live you have no worries

If you die you only have two worries.

Do you go to Heaven or to Hell?

If you go to Heaven you have no worries.

If you go to Hell you are too busy catching up with family and friends to have any worries.

The Magician and the Elf

While riding one day, a magician met an Elf riding along with a dog
and a sheep and began a conversation.

Magician: "Hey, nice dog you got there. Mind if I speak to him?"

Elf: "My dog doesn't talk."

Magician: "Hey dog, how's it going?"

Dog: "Doin' alright."

Elf: Look of shock.

Magician: "Is this Elf your owner?" pointing at the Elf.

Dog: "Yep"

Magician: "How does he treat you?"

Dog: "Real good. He walks me twice a day, feeds me great food, and takes me to the lake once a week to play."

Elf: Look of total disbelief.

Magician: "Mind if I talk to your horse?"

Elf: "My horse does not talk."

Magician: "Hey horse, how's it going?"

Horse: "Cool."

Elf: look of shock.

Magician: "Is this your owner? " pointing at the Elf.

Horse: "Yes"

Magician: "How's he treat you?"

Horse: "Pretty good, thanks for asking. He rides me regularly, brushes
me down often, and keeps me in a shed to protect me."

Elf: more amazement.

Magician: "Mind if I talk to your sheep?"

Elf: "My sheep is a liar."

The Great Writer

There was once a young man who, in his youth, professed his desire to become a great writer. When asked to define "great" he said,

"I want to write stuff that the whole world will read, I want to write stuff that people will react to on a truly emotional level. I want to write stuff that will make them scream and cry and howl in pain and anger!"

He now works for Microsoft, writing error messages.

Mummy Mummy

Mummy Mummy jokes originated in ancient Egypt. Here are the top five and some of the also-rans.

1

Mummy Mummy what is a vampire?

Shut up and drink your soup before it clots.

2

Mummy Mummy are you sure this is the right way to bake a cake?

Shut up and get back in the oven

3

Mummy Mummy I hate daddy's guts.

Then leave them on the side of the plate dear

4

Mummy can I lick the bowl?

No pull the chain like everyone else.

5

Mummy Mummy why am I walking round in circles?

Shut up or I'll nail the other foot to the floor.

Also rans

Mummy Mummy Andy called me a boat.

A boat dear?

Well he said I was a little ship.

Mummy Mummy what's a werewolf

Shut up and comb your face.

Mummy Mummy can I play with Spot?

No dear that's six times we've dug him up this week.

Mummy Mummy where did the baby come from?

Mary, I told you we found him under a gooseberry bush.

Is that why he's still got a thorn stuck in him?

You are addicted to the net if

> Your cat has its own Facebook page.
>
> The last girl you picked up was a jpeg.
>
> You start tilting your head sideways to smile.
>
> You turn on your computer and turn off your wife.
>
> When your car crashes you try to press CTRL ALT and DEL

Your wife asks for sex and you ask her to switch on her webcam.

You don't know what sex your closest friends are

You'd rather go to http://www.weather.com/ than look out your window.

Knock knock...who's there

Duane
Duane who
Duane the bath, I'm dwowning.

Felix
Felix who
Felix my ice cream again I'll smash his face in.

Granny

Knock knock
who's there?
Granny
Knock knock
who's there?
Granny
Knock knock
who's there?
Aunt
Aunt who?
Aunt you glad I got rid of all those grannies?

Gove

A plastic surgeon and former Education Secretary Michael Gove met at a party. Eventually Gove asked the plastic surgeon what he did for a living.
"Well you might say I tuck up your features."

"What a co-incidence," said Gove, "I do just the opposite."

Politicians

How do you save a politician from drowning?

Well you could take your foot off its head.

But don't :-)

This Christmas - What do you give the politician who has

everything?

You could give a course of antibiotics.

But don't :-)

How do you tell the head of OFSTED from a narrow-minded little nazi

with a bug up its butt the size of an emu?

(No answer has been found to this one)

Why do politicians never win at football?

Too busy moving the goalposts.

Royal College of Psychiatry

What follows is in bad taste.

If you are offended by bad taste please read it carefully so you can be properly offended and then complain that you find it offensive :-)

(If you have read it before please read it again so you can complain you have read it before)

A transcript of the new answering service recently installed at the Royal College of Psychiatry:

"Hello, and welcome to the mental health hotline:

If you are obsessive-compulsive, press 1 repeatedly.

If you are codependent, please ask someone to press 2 for you.

If you have multiple personalities, press 3, 4, 5 and 6.

If you are paranoid, we know who you are and what you want. Stay on the line so we can trace your call,

If you are delusional, press 7 and your call will be transferred to the mother ship.

If you are schizophrenic, listen carefully and a small voice will tell you which number to press.

If you are a manic-depressive, it doesn't matter which number you press, no-one will answer.

If you are dyslexic, press 9696969696969.

If you have a nervous disorder, please fidget with the hash key until a representative comes on the line.

If you have amnesia press 8 and state your name, address, phone, date of birth, social security number and your mother's maiden name.

If you have bi-polar disorder, please leave a message after the beep or before the beep. Or after the beep. Please wait for the beep.

If you have short-term memory loss, press 9. If you have short-term memory loss, press 9. If you have short-term memory loss, press 9. If you have short-term memory loss, press 9.

If you have low self-esteem, please hang up. All our operators are too busy to talk to you."

Scunthorpe

A government agency in Scunthorpe added a filtering program to their computers which prevented any emails with profanities in them from getting through. After a week they realised that none at all were getting through.

That was an agency in Scunthorpe.

Paul McMillan

Signs of the Times

In a Bangkok temple: "IT IS FORBIDDEN TO ENTER A WOMAN, EVEN A FOREIGNER, IF DRESSED AS A MAN."

Cocktail lounge, Norway: "LADIES ARE REQUESTED NOT TO HAVE CHILDREN IN THE BAR."

At a Budapest zoo: "PLEASE DO NOT FEED THE ANIMALS. IF YOU HAVE ANY SUITABLE FOOD, GIVE IT TO THE GUARD ON DUTY."

Doctors office, Rome: "SPECIALIST IN WOMEN AND OTHER DISEASES."

Hotel, Acapulco: "THE MANAGER HAS PERSONALLY PASSED ALL THE WATER SERVED HERE."

Dry cleaners, Bangkok: "DROP YOUR TROUSERS HERE FOR THE BEST RESULTS."

In a Nairobi restaurant: "CUSTOMERS WHO FIND OUR WAITRESSES RUDE OUGHT TO SEE THE MANAGER."

On the grounds of a private school: "NO TRESPASSING WITHOUT PERMISSION."

On an Athi River highway: "TAKE NOTICE: WHEN THIS SIGN IS UNDER WATER, THIS ROAD IS IMPASSABLE."

On a poster at Kencom: "ARE YOU AN ADULT THAT CANNOT READ? IF SO, WE CAN HELP."

In a City restaurant: "OPEN SEVEN DAYS A WEEK AND WEEKENDS."

One of the Mathare buildings: "MENTAL HEALTH PREVENTION CENTRE."

A sign seen on an automatic hand dryer: "DO NOT ACTIVATE WITH WET HANDS."

In a Pumwani maternity ward: "NO CHILDREN ALLOWED."

In a cemetery: "PERSONS ARE PROHIBITED FROM PICKING FLOWERS FROM ANY BUT THEIR OWN GRAVES."

Tokyo hotel's rules and regulations: "GUESTS ARE REQUESTED NOT TO SMOKE OR DO OTHER DISGUSTING BEHAVIOURS IN BED."

On the menu of a Swiss restaurant: "OUR WINES LEAVE YOU NOTHING TO HOPE FOR."

In a Tokyo bar: "SPECIAL COCKTAILS FOR THE LADIES WITH NUTS."

Hotel brochure, Italy: "THIS HOTEL IS RENOWNED FOR ITS PEACE AND SOLITUDE. IN FACT, CROWDS FROM ALL OVER THE WORLD FLOCK HERE TO ENJOY ITS SOLITUDE."

Hotel lobby, Bucharest: "THE LIFT IS BEING FIXED FOR THE NEXT DAY. DURING THAT TIME WE REGRET THAT YOU WILL BE UNBEARABLE."

Hotel elevator, Paris: "PLEASE LEAVE YOUR VALUES AT THE FRONT DESK."

Hotel, Yugoslavia: "THE FLATTENING OF UNDERWEAR WITH PLEASURE IS THE JOB OF THE CHAMBERMAID."

Hotel, Japan: "YOU ARE INVITED TO TAKE ADVANTAGE OF THE CHAMBERMAID."

In the lobby of a Moscow hotel across from a Russian Orthodox monastery: "YOU ARE WELCOME TO VISIT THE CEMETERY WHERE FAMOUS RUSSIAN AND SOVIET COMPOSERS, ARTISTS, AND WRITERS ARE BURIED DAILY EXCEPT THURSDAY."

Taken from a menu, Poland: "SALAD A FIRM'S OWN MAKE; LIMPID RED BEET SOUP WITH CHEESY DUMPLINGS IN THE FORM OF A FINGER; ROASTED DUCK LET LOOSE; BEEF RASHERS BEATEN IN THE COUNTRY PEOPLE'S FASHION."

Supermarket, Hong Kong: "FOR YOUR CONVENIENCE, WE RECOMMEND COURTEOUS, EFFICIENT SELF-SERVICE."

From the "Soviet Weekly": "THERE WILL BE A MOSCOW EXHIBITION OF ARTS BY 15,000 SOVIET REPUBLIC PAINTERS AND SCULPTORS. THESE WERE EXECUTED OVER THE PAST TWO YEARS."

In an East African newspaper: "A NEW SWIMMING POOL IS RAPIDLY TAKING SHAPE SINCE THE CONTRACTORS HAVE THROWN IN THE BULK OF THEIR WORKERS."

Hotel, Vienna: "IN CASE OF FIRE, DO YOUR UTMOST TO ALARM THE HOTEL PORTER."

A sign posted in Germany's Black Forest: "IT IS STRICTLY FORBIDDEN ON OUR BLACK FOREST CAMPING SITE THAT PEOPLE OF DIFFERENT SEX, FOR INSTANCE, MEN AND WOMEN, LIVE TOGETHER IN ONE TENT UNLESS THEY ARE MARRIED WITH EACH OTHER FOR THIS PURPOSE."

Hotel, Zurich: BECAUSE OF THE IMPROPRIETY OF ENTERTAINING GUESTS OF THE OPPOSITE SEX IN THE BEDROOM, IT IS SUGGESTED THAT THE LOBBY BE USED FOR THIS PURPOSE."

The unrepeatable limerick

Robin came home from work laughing. All through dinner he was giggling and quietly chortled while they were watching TV. At bedtime Marion was so intrigued that she really needed to know what was so funny.

"No I am sorry. There was this limerick John told me and I am afraid it was so disgusting that I cannot repeat it to you."

Marion said that she was fairly broadminded and she could cope with most things.

Robin said he knew that already but this really was beyond the pale.

Marion said she didn't mind now if it was completely outrageous if it was as funny as it seemed.

Robin repeated that he knew she would not normally mind a bit of smut but this really was the outside of enough, but just so very funny.

Well Marion got really persuasive and eventually Robin agreed that he would tell her the limerick but he would cut out the really disgusting parts and only leave in the parts which Marion would not find just too too shocking.

"Blank Blank Blank Blank Blank Blank Blank Blank

Who Blank Blank Blank Blank Blank Blank Blank

Blank Blank Blank Blank Blank

And Blank Blank Blank Blank

Blank Blank Blank Blank Blank Blank Blank Fuck."

Sadness at the funeral

What with all the sadness and trauma going on in the world at the moment, it is worth reflecting on the death of a very important person which almost went unnoticed last week. Larry La Prise, the man who wrote "The Hokey Kokey" died peacefully aged 83. The most traumatic part for his family was getting him into the coffin. They put his left leg in - and things just started to go downhill from there.

Vienna or Berlin?

I do not know if this is a Viennese joke or a Berlin joke. You will have to judge.

You are lost in the street and you ask for directions to the railway station.

The Berliner will give you precise instructions on how to get there and if necessary the times of the trains. If you offer thanks the reply will be, "Never mind the thanks. REPEAT THE INSTRUCTIONS."

The Viennese will talk to you in a charming and entertaining way for at least half an hour before regretfully admitting complete ignorance of the whereabouts of the railway station.

Incidentally, according to the great Eddie Izzard, when Kennedy declaimed "Ich bin ein Berliner" this meant "I am a doughnut." In this instance I mean an inhabitant of Berlin because I cannot advocate talking to doughnuts.

Shaggy Camel Story

(Only read this if you think you have the time)

Amir the camel driver was given a task by the Sultan. The Sultan was minded to take a wife and had in mind the beautiful princess Saralinda who dwelt on the far side of the great bled.

It was Amir's task to lead twelve camels laden with gifts across the great bled to the Princess Saralinda from the Sultan.

Day after day of burning sun beating down on the endless sands of the great bled passed. In time Amir began to hear, or to think he heard, a voice. And the voice seemed to Amir the camel driver to be counting 1, 2, 3, 4, 5, 6, 7…and other numbers as well.

Amir the camel driver was a patient man, as one who drives camels across the great bled for a living has to be really…and as one who reads this tale also has to be.

Patient that is. Being a man is of course optional. Well not exactly optional but patience is essential.

Amir the camel driver was, as I said before, a patient man. Yet as the days of burning sun beating down on the endless sands of the great bled passed, even the heart of the patient Amir was turned to wrath by the voice which seemed to fill his waking and his sleeping thoughts with its counting 1, 2, 3, 4, 5, 6, 7...and other numbers as well.

In time he came to eye even the very camels with suspicion. He strode purposefully down the line of twelve camels and looked into the eyes of each camel in turn. It was when he reached the twelfth and final camel that the camel winked, or at any rate that is how Amir the camel driver tells the story.

The reader should be aware that Amir is living yet and can be seen in the oasis of Peckham.

Amir took his long and very sharp camel-driver's knife out and slit the throat of the camel, spilling its blood onto the sands of the great bled.

The caravan (now of course you should not think of caravan parks and Bognor Regis when I mention caravans because of course this just refers to a group of twelve ...or in the present circumstances eleven...camels crossing the golden sands of the great bled under the merciless glare of the hot sun. The caravan as so designated went peacefully on its way.

Day after day of burning sun beating down on the endless sands of the great bled passed. In time Amir began again to hear, or to think he heard, a voice. And the voice seemed to Amir the camel driver to be counting 1, 2, 3, 4, 5, 6, 7...and other numbers as well.

Amir stalked dramatically down the long line of the camels and when he reached the eleventh and final camel, he saw, or he thinks he saw or he *says* that he thinks he saw the camel wink at him. In a frenzy this normally placid camel-driver slit the throat of the camel and spilt its blood on the sand. After this for a while they continued peacefully with only the silence of the great bled for company.

Day after day of burning sun beating down on the endless sands of the great bled passed. In time Amir began again to hear, or to think he heard, a voice. And the voice seemed to Amir the camel driver to be counting 1, 2, 3, 4, 5, 6, 7...and other numbers as well.

Amir stalked dramatically down the long line of the camels and when he reached the tenth and final camel, he saw, or he thinks he saw or he *says* that he thinks he saw the camel wink at him. In a frenzy this normally placid camel-driver slit the throat of the camel and spilt its blood on the sand. After this for a while they continued peacefully with only the silence of the great bled for company.

Day after day of burning sun beating down on the endless sands of the great bled passed. In time Amir began again to hear, or to think he heard, a voice. And the voice seemed to Amir the camel driver to be counting 1, 2, 3, 4, 5, 6, 7...and other numbers as well.

Amir stalked dramatically down the long line of the camels and when he reached the ninth and final camel, he saw, or he thinks he saw or he *says* that he thinks he saw the camel wink at him. In a frenzy this normally placid camel-driver slit the throat of the camel and spilt its blood on the sand. After this for a while they continued peacefully with only the silence of the great bled for company.

Day after day of burning sun beating down on the endless sands of the great bled passed. In time Amir began again to hear, or to think he heard, a voice. And the voice seemed to Amir the camel driver to be counting 1, 2, 3, 4, 5, 6, 7...and other numbers as well.

Amir stalked dramatically down the long line of the camels and when he reached the eighth and final camel, he saw, or he thinks he saw or he *says* that he thinks he saw the camel wink at him. In a frenzy this normally placid camel-driver slit the throat of the camel and spilt its blood on the sand. After this for a while they continued peacefully with only the silence of the great bled for company.

Day after day of burning sun beating down on the endless sands of the great bled passed. In time Amir began again to hear, or to think he heard, a voice. And the voice seemed to Amir the camel driver to be counting 1, 2, 3, 4, 5, 6, 7...and other numbers as well.

Amir stalked dramatically down the long line of the camels and when he reached the seventh and final camel, he saw, or he thinks he saw or he *says* that he thinks he saw the camel wink at him. In a frenzy this normally placid camel-driver slit the throat of the camel and spilt its blood on the sand. After this for a while they continued peacefully with only the silence of the great bled for company.

Day after day of burning sun beating down on the endless sands of the great bled passed. In time Amir began again to hear, or to think he heard, a voice. And the voice seemed to Amir the camel driver to be counting 1, 2, 3, 4, 5, 6, 7...and other numbers as well.

Amir stalked dramatically down the long line of the camels and when he reached the sixth and final camel, he saw, or he thinks he saw or he *says* that he thinks he saw the camel wink at him. In a frenzy this normally placid camel-driver slit the throat of the camel and spilt its blood on the sand. After this for a while they continued peacefully with only the silence of the great bled for company.

Day after day of burning sun beating down on the endless sands of the great bled passed. In time Amir began again to hear, or to think he heard, a voice. And the voice seemed to Amir the camel driver to be counting 1, 2, 3, 4, 5, 6, 7...and other numbers as well.

Amir stalked dramatically down the long line of the camels and when he reached the fifth and final camel, he saw, or he thinks he saw or he *says* that he thinks he saw the camel wink at him. In a frenzy this normally placid camel-driver slit the throat of the camel and spilt its blood on the sand. After this for a while they continued peacefully with only the silence of the great bled for company.

Day after day of burning sun beating down on the endless sands of the great bled passed. In time Amir began again to hear, or to think he heard, a voice. And the voice seemed to Amir the camel driver to be counting 1, 2, 3, 4, 5, 6, 7...and other numbers as well.

Amir stalked dramatically down the long line of the camels and when he reached the fourth and final camel, he saw, or he thinks he saw or he *says* that he thinks he saw the camel wink at him. In a frenzy this normally placid camel-driver slit the throat of the camel and spilt its blood on the sand. After this for a while they continued peacefully with only the silence of the great bled for company.

Day after day of burning sun beating down on the endless sands of the great bled passed. In time Amir began again to hear, or to think he heard, a voice. And the voice seemed to Amir the camel driver to be counting 1, 2, 3, 4, 5, 6, 7...and other numbers as well.

Amir stalked dramatically down the not quite so long line of the camels and when he reached the third and final camel, he saw, or he thinks he saw or he *says* that he thinks he saw the camel wink at him. In a frenzy this normally placid camel-driver slit the throat of the camel and spilt its blood on the sand. After this for a while they continued peacefully with only the silence of the great bled for company.

Day followed day of burning sun beating down on the endless sands of the great bled. In time Amir began again to hear, or to think he heard, a voice. And the voice seemed to Amir the camel driver to be counting 1, 2, 3, 4, 5, 6, 7...and other numbers as well.

Amir stalked dramatically down the very short line of the camels and when he reached the second and final camel, he saw, or he thinks he saw or he *says* that he thinks he saw the camel wink at him. In a frenzy this normally placid camel-driver slit the throat of the camel and spilt its blood on the sand. After this for a while they continued peacefully with only the silence of the great bled for company.

Not a cloud crossed the sky as day after day of burning sun beating down on the endless sands of the great bled passed. In time Amir began again to hear, or to think he heard, a voice. And the voice seemed to Amir the camel driver to be counting 1, 2, 3, 4, 5, 6, 7...and other numbers as well.

Amir stalked dramatically towards the final camel, he saw, or he thinks he saw or he *says* that he thinks he saw the camel wink at him. In a frenzy this normally placid (though not recently so to be fair) camel-driver slit the throat of the camel and spilt its blood on the sand. After this for a while he continued peacefully with only the silence of the great bled and his own heavy breathing for company.

Eventually Amir the camel driver arrived at the gates of the castle of the princess Saralinda and he was able to tell her in great detail of the diamonds and emeralds and rubies and precious gifts of the sultan which he had left in the trackless wastes of the great bled and to offer his apologies for not actually bringing them.

And in response the princess Saralinda said

> **"It's the thought that counts."**

Comeback all is forgiven

> Why do people hate me at first sight?
> It saves time.

> Can I have this dance?
> Certainly. I don't want it.

> Do you suffer fools gladly?
> Well I'm talking to you aren't I?

What do you want for Christmas?

> According to legend, the British Ambassador to Washington was asked this question by a journalist when he first arrived in post. The journalist had also rung the other embassies with the same question.

The next day in a seasonal piece, the newspaper reported that the Soviet Ambassador wanted an end to nuclear proliferation (which rather dates this story!) The French Ambassador wanted world peace and the British Ambassador wanted a bottle of scotch.

Of course the fact of the matter is that the British Ambassador had a reasonable chance of getting a bottle of scotch.

Yes Sir That's my baby!

The following are all replies that British women have put on Child Support Agency forms in the section for listing father's details:

These are genuine excerpts from the forms. (It says here! I have my doubts as to whether they are genuine but they are genuinely funny anyway)

01. Regarding the identity of the father of my twins, child A was fathered by J** M******. I am unsure as to the identity of the father of child B, but I believe that he was conceived on the same night.

02. I am unsure as to the identity of the father of my child as I was being sick out of a window when taken unexpectedly from behind. I can provide you with a list of names of men that I think were at the party if this helps.

03. I do not know the name of the father of my little girl. She was conceived at a party at 3600 Grand Avenue where I had unprotected sex with a man I met that night. I do remember that the sex was so good that I fainted. If you do manage to track down the father, can you send me his phone number? Thanks.

04. I don't know the identity of the father of my daughter. He drives a BMW that now has a hole made by my stiletto in one of the door rear panels. Perhaps you can contact BMW service stations in this area and see if he's had it replaced.

05. I have never had sex with a man. I am awaiting a letter from the Pope confirming that my son's conception was immaculate and that he is Christ risen again.

06. I cannot tell you the name of child A's dad as he informs me that to do so would blow his cover and that would have cataclysmic implications for the British economy. I am torn between doing right by you and right by the country. Please advise.

07. I do not know who the father of my child was as all squaddies look the same to me. I can confirm that he was a Royal Green Jacket.

08. Peter Smith is the father of child A. If you do catch up with him can you ask him what he did with my AC/DC CDs?

09. From the dates it seems that my daughter was conceived at EuroDisney. Maybe it really is the Magic Kingdom.

10. So much about that night is a blur. The only thing that I remember for sure is Delia Smith did a program about eggs earlier in the evening. If I'd have stayed in and watched more TV rather than going to the party at 146 Miller Drive, mine might have remained unfertilized.

11. I am unsure as to the identity of the father of my baby, after all when you eat a can of beans you can't be sure which one made you fart.

The Doctor, the architect and the politician

A doctor, an architect and a politician were discussing which of their professions was the oldest.

"Well in Genesis, it says that God created Eve from Adam's collar bone. That is clearly a medical procedure." said the Doctor

"Ah yes but before that God created order out of chaos. That is why he is called the architect of the universe." said the architect.

"And who do you think created the chaos?" smirked the politician.

Skinheads

There was a young skinhead from Ealing

Who got on a bus in Dahjeling

The sign on the door

said "Don't spit on the floor",

So he turned round and spat on the ceiling

A comment I remember from the 1960s was "you never see a skinhead in a fight" (wait for incredulous response before continuing) "Skinheads but never a skinhead."

I think it safe to say this now because most of the skinheads are my age and some, ironically, going bald.

Odd one-liners

MI5 have been issued with copies of the Human Rights Act. They use them to wipe their backsides.

My neighbour asked if he could pick my brains. How was I to know he was a zombie?

It is not widely known that Nigel Farage is an expert on the ancient British custom of bear-baiting. In fact his aides call him the master baiter.

Madonna got a piggy back from Nigel Farage. I told her, "Donna this is like a virgin on the ridiculous."

I went to a meeting of my Premature Ejaculation Help Group this morning, but it turns out it was tomorrow.

According to Descartes if triangles had a God it would be three-sided. If Gove had a God it would be one-sided.

The Thatcher Foundation is donating a billion dollars to a program to breed smaller camels and a further billion to a project manufacturing giant needles

In Sainsbury's

"Thank God for Sainsbury's. They keep the riffraff out of Waitrose" as Stephen Fry put it.

And thank God for Waitrose, they keeps the snobs out of Sainsbury's.

I joined a queue in the supermarket and I spotted Tony Blair in the queue. Imagine my surprise when I saw Ed Miliband was in front of him, then Nick Clegg, Jeremy Clarkson and David Cameron.

Then I noticed that the queue was "baskets only."

(The original version of this had Paul Daniels, Jimmy Saville, Edward Heath and Harold Wilson - you can basically make up your own list!)

A man walked into a bar

A man walked into a bar

He turned to his mate and said "Come on, name your poison."

His mate said, "you must get your eyes checked, this is the chemists."

A man walked into a bar

He walked up to the barman and asked,

"How tall do penguins get?"

The barman asked around the bar they came up with a consensus that generally they are about 3 feet maximum.

The guy looked really worried.

"I was hoping they might get a lot taller than that. I think I just ran over a nun."

A man walked into a bar

He went over to the piano and he produced a little man (oh no not this joke? Yes it is) He was about a foot tall and then he started running up and down the piano keyboard, leaping from note to note and playing a variety of tunes.

"Tell me," said a curious bystander, "If I buy you a pint will you tell me how you came across this remarkable chap?"

The man agreed and over a pint he said,

"Well an old lady was in difficulties in the street, she was a bit doddery and I was able to help her to get home. She claimed that she was a witch. Well this later proved to be true. She asked me what I wanted most in the world and that is how I came by this little chap.

"The thing was, I think she was a bit hard of hearing and she thought I had asked her for a twelve-inch pianist."

Pothole ahoy!

The system for reporting potholes - and God knows there are plenty of them - is interesting.

I went to the Worthing website. They said "nothing to do with us, go to West Sussex". You can't report it to Worthing so they can automatically forward it to the relevant department. That would be helping and believe me they are not there to help.

West Sussex of course said "nothing to do with us, go to the oddly named website "lovewestsussex". It is not a dating site.

I tried to report a pothole. "Ah Mr McMillan, have you got an account?" Why in the name of sanity do I need an account? I only want to report a pothole.

No you need an account.

OKAY (sigh) apply for an account. They emailed me - eventually - and gave me an eight-character password. They wont let you choose your own password of course. You have to put up with their password and GET IT RIGHT if you want to report a pothole.

Do you still want to report a pothole or have you lost the will to live yet?

And then of course they need your mobile phone number before you can proceed. And if you haven't got a mobile phone? Well obviously if you haven't got a mobile phone you have no pothole QED.

I eventually managed to report the pothole. Now lets see if they do anything about it.

You have two cows

This is a variation on a joke I remember from the 1950s. It has been updated a bit and is perhaps a trifle long now. Still worth it though.

SOCIALISM

You have 2 cows.

You give one to your neighbour

COMMUNISM

You have 2 cows.

The State takes both and gives you some milk

NAZISM

You have 2 cows.

The State takes both and shoots you

BUREAUCRATISM

You have 2 cows.

The State takes both, shoots one, milks the other, and then

throws the milk away

VENTURE CAPITALISM

You have two cows.

You sell three of them to your publicly listed company, using letters of credit opened by your brother-in-law at the bank, then execute a debt/equity swap with an associated general offer so that you get all four cows back, with a tax exemption

for five cows.

The milk rights of the six cows are transferred via an intermediary to a Cayman Island Company secretly owned by the majority shareholder who sells the rights to all seven cows back to your listed company.

The annual report says the company owns eight cows, with an option on one more. You sell one cow to buy a new president of the United States , leaving you with nine cows. No balance sheet provided with the release.

The public then buys your bull.

SURREALISM

You have two giraffes.

The government requires you to take harmonica lessons.

AN AMERICAN CORPORATION

You have two cows.

You sell one, and force the other to produce the milk of four cows.

Later, you hire a consultant to analyse why the cow has dropped dead.

A JAPANESE CORPORATION

You have two cows.

You redesign them so they are one-tenth the size of an ordinary cow and produce twenty times the milk.

You then create a clever cow cartoon image called a Cowkimona and

market it worldwide.

A SWISS CORPORATION

You have 5000 cows. None of them belong to you.

You charge the owners for storing them.

A CHINESE CORPORATION

You have two cows.

You have 300 people milking them.

You claim that you have full employment, and high bovine productivity.

You arrest the newsman who reported the real situation.

AN INDIAN CORPORATION

You have two cows.

You worship them.

A BRITISH CORPORATION

You have two cows.

Both are mad.

AN IRAQI CORPORATION

Everyone thinks you have lots of cows.

You tell them that you have none.

No-one believes you, so they bomb the ** out of you and invade your country.

You still have no cows, but at least you are now a Democracy.

AN AUSTRALIAN CORPORATION

You have two cows.

Business seems pretty good.

You close the office and go for a few beers to celebrate.

A NEW ZEALAND CORPORATION

You have two cows.

The one on the left looks very attractive...

Not lightbulbs. Anything but the lightbulbs

How many behaviourists does it take to change a lightbulb?

Just the one but it really has to want to change.

How many Freudians?

Two. One to screw the mother ... I mean bulb and one to hold the penis...ladder.

Oh my God

Three Plymouth Brethren died and naturally enough went to heaven. St Peter met them and looked a little awkward. In the end he said,

"There's a couple of things you need to know about God. To start with, she's black."

Happy Christmas

Rudolf Nureyev and Margot Fonteyn were looking out of the window.

"Look darling it's snowing."

"No darling its raining."

"I tell you it's snowing."

"Listen, Rudolf the red knows rain dear!"

> If you enjoyed reading this,
>
> what exactly is the matter with you?

Printed in the USA
CPSIA information can be obtained
at www.ICGtesting.com
LVHW020513040624
782215LV00008B/411